A Guide to Kotlikoff, Moeller and Solman's

Get What's Yours:

The Secrets to Maxing Out

Your Social Security

———

Summary and Critique,

Key Ideas and Facts

by

I.K. Mullins

Brief, Concise and to the Point
Publishing

A Guide to Kotlikoff, Moeller and Solman's

Get What's Yours

A Guide to Kotlikoff, Moeller and Solman's Get What's Yours: The Secrets to Maxing Out Your Social Security — Summary and Critique, Key Ideas and Facts

ISBN-13: 978-1511519168

ISBN-10: 1511519169

www.ideas-facts-books.com

Disclaimer

This is not the actual Kotlikoff, Moeller and Solman's *Get What's Yours: The Secrets to Maxing Out Your Social Security*. The primary objective of this book is to bring insightful discussion and critique of Kotlikoff, Moeller and Solman's *Get What's Yours: The Secrets to Maxing Out Your Social Security* to readers everywhere.

The publisher and author of this book make no representations or warranties with respect to the accuracy or completeness of these contents and disclaim all warranties. The publisher or author of this book is not liable for any damages whatsoever. This book is not endorsed or affiliated with Kotlikoff, Moeller and Solman, or any person or entity associated with their book, *Get What's Yours: The Secrets to Maxing Out Your Social Security*. Do not purchase this BOOK if you are looking for a full copy of Kotlikoff, Moeller and Solman's *Get What's Yours: The Secrets to Maxing Out Your Social Security*.

A Guide to Kotlikoff, Moeller and Solman's

Get What's Yours

Table of Contents

Preface 7

Introduction..10

Part I. Summary and Analysis of the Key Ideas in *Get What's Yours* 16

1. The Past and Present of the Social Security Program..21

Analysis and Comments on the Past and Present of the Social Security Program.............22

2. The Best Strategies for Collecting Social Security Benefits 24

Analysis and Comments on the Best Strategies 30

3. Spousal Benefits, Divorced Spousal Benefits, Widower Benefits 35

Analysis and Comments on Spousal and Survivor Benefits..39

4. Disability Benefits...43

Analysis and Comments on Disability Benefits 44

5. *Gay Married Couples Benefits* *46*

Analysis and Comments on Gay Marriage Benefits 47

6. *The Earnings Test and Its Impact on Benefits* .*48*

Analysis and Comments on the Earnings Test and Its Impact on Benefits 50

7. *Social Security "Gotchas"* *51*

Analysis and Comments on the Social Security "Gotchas" 54

Part II. A Critique of the Principal Messages in *Get What's Yours* **58**

1. *The Future of the Social Security Program* *59*

2. *Social Security and Economic Inequality* *63*

3. *Social Security Benefits and Real Inflation* *66*

4. *The Real Value of Kotlikoff's Book* *72*

References **74**

A Guide to Kotlikoff, Moeller and Solman's

Get What's Yours

Preface

Social Security, a US federal program of social insurance and benefits, pays out hundreds of billions of dollars every year. It is one of the largest government programs in the world, and it is a very convoluted program. Social Security benefit rules are difficult to navigate and understand. For married couples, for example, the formula for each spouse's benefit involves 10 mathematical functions. Overall, the Social Security system includes 2,728 core rules and thousands of additional instructions in its Program Operating Manual (the additional instructions are supposed to elucidate the core rules). Their printed version is longer than the printed version of the Federal Tax Code.

While the Social Security system has become more and more complex, its staff and resources have been shrinking. The number of Social Security employees was recently cut by 11,000 positions. Today, approximately 75,000 Social Security workers have to handle benefits for about 56 million Americans, and many Social Security representatives are not trained well enough to help retirees navigate Social Security benefits. This is why people who have already retired, and people who plan to retire, should be cautious about taking advice from Social Security representatives.

Laurence Kotlikoff, Phillip Moeller and Paul Solman wrote a book, *Get What's Yours: The Secrets to Maxing Out Your Social Security*, that explains basic strategies for navigating the Social Security system and maximizing a household's Social Security retirement, as well as spousal, child, parent, survivor, divorcee and disability benefits. Kotlikoff, Moeller and Solman explain in their book how "file and suspend" (applying for benefits and not taking them) and "start, stop, start" (starting benefits, stopping them and restarting benefits) strategies can help people get more money out of Social Security. Their book also discusses the pitfalls in the Social Security benefit system that people should avoid.

This book, *A Guide to Kotlikoff, Moeller and Solman's Get What's Yours: The Secrets to Maxing Out Your Social Security Summary and Critique, Key Ideas and Facts*, includes an unofficial summary and analysis of the key ideas of Kotlikoff, Moeller and

Solman's book, *Get What's Yours: The Secrets to Maxing Out Your Social Security*, as well as a critique of its principal messages . Moreover, this *Guide* goes beyond the information included in Kotlikoff, Moeller and Solman's book and reviews other selected studies and data related to the present and future of Social Security benefits.

Introduction

Today, a typical American saves less than 10,000 dollars by the time he or she is 10 years from retiring. Rising costs of living, as well as the rising costs of medical expenses, can easily force many people to outlive their not-so-big savings, therefore making Social Security benefits crucial for the survival of millions of Americans. According to the Center on Budget and Policy Priorities, Social Security benefits remain the major source of cash income for almost 70 percent of American retirees. The average monthly benefit—1,217 US dollars—does not seem like a large amount of money, but it keeps approximately 14 million older Americans out of poverty.

The history of the emergence and evolution of Social Security goes all the way back to 1929, the year when the US stock market crashed. After the crash in October 1929, the US stock market lost 40 percent of its value within three months, erasing 26 billion dollars of wealth. While the US was slipping into the Great Depression, unemployment exceeded 25 percent, approximately 10,000 banks failed, millions of people became unemployed. These dire circumstances called for change. Many proposals have been made to address the situation.

For example, Huey Long, who was Governor of Louisiana from 1928 to 1932 and elected to the US Senate in 1930, wanted the government to confiscate the wealth of the nation's rich. His program, which was called Share Our Wealth, required the federal government to provide every family with an annual income of $5,000, limit private fortunes to 50 million dollars, legacies to 5 million dollars, and annual incomes to 1 million dollars. Under this program, everyone over age 60 would get paid a pension. By 1935, the program had 7.7 million supporters.

In order to deal with the rising economic problems, Workers Compensation programs and welfare programs for the elderly were created at the state level. Then, on June 8, 1934, President Franklin D. Roosevelt announced his intention to provide a nation-wide program for Social Security. He created the Committee on Economic Security (CES) that had to study the problem of economic insecurity and to provide recommendations for its solution. In January 1935, the CES made its report to the President, and, on August 14, 1935, President Roosevelt signed the Social Security Act into law. In addition to Social Security, it included unemployment insurance, aid to dependent children, old-age assistance, as well as grants to the states to provide medical care.

Today, Social Security offers various types of benefits to Americans: retirement benefits; spousal benefits; spousal benefits for those who care for an eligible child or children; child benefits for the young children of retirees; child benefits for disabled children of retirees; divorcee spousal benefits; widow or widower survivor benefits; divorcee widow or widower survivor benefits; parental benefits; survivor benefits to young children; survivor benefits to disabled children regardless of age; and disability benefits.

Any American who has worked in "covered" employment for 40 quarters of a year (i.e., 10 years in total, and those 40 quarters are not required to be consecutive) is eligible for Social Security benefits. By "covered" employment, Social Security understands those jobs where Social Security taxes (FICA contributions) are deducted from a person's employee compensation. The Social Security tax applies to wage or self-employment income that is equal to or less than the "tax max," which changes with time. In 2015, the tax max is 118,500 dollars.

Moreover, if a person is qualified for Social Security benefits, then his or her current spouse, ex-spouse(s), young children, disabled children and parents may also be eligible to receive certain Social Security benefits (even if they have never worked and never paid the Social Security tax). When the person dies, the person's work record can also make his or her survivors eligible to receive Social Security benefits.

Social Security is intended to help people who reach their retirement age, as well as their relatives. However, Kotlikoff, Moeller and Solman argue that the Social Security program is not fair. It describes its benefit rules using confusing language; it provides complicated instructions that are often difficult to understand; and it allows those beneficiaries who are better educated about the Social Security system's rules to get more benefits than other beneficiaries.

It is not a surprise then that Kotlikoff, Moeller and Solman's book has become a national bestseller. In their book, the authors list 50 secrets to getting higher benefits. They also draw readers' attention to pitfalls (gotchas) that can cost retirees lots of money. The primary objective of Kotlikoff, Moeller and Solman's book is to help all beneficiaries understand the Social Security jargon and learn how to get the most out of the system.

The authors of *Get What's Yours: The Secrets to Maxing Out Your Social Security* are certainly experts in questions of retirement and Social Security benefits. Laurence Kotlikoff is a professor of economics at Boston University. Philip Moeller writes about retirement for *Money Magazine*, the PBS website's Making Sen$e, and other news outlets. Paul Solman is a business and economics correspondent for *The PBS NewsHour*. The idea of the book came to them when they were discussing their own retirement planning. Their discussion brought up their concerns about the complexity of the Social Security system. Then, they decided to write a book that would tell Americans how to maximize their retirement benefits and how to avoid some traps that exist in the system.

Part I. Summary and Analysis of the Key Ideas in *Get What's Yours*

When it comes to the Social Security, there are many important terms that people have to know in order to navigate the benefits system:

- **Eligible**—the Social Security system uses the term "eligible" to describe a person who is qualified due to age or some other circumstances to file and collect benefits.
- **Entitled**—the Social Security system uses the term "entitled" when referring to a person who has already filed for benefits and is collecting benefits.
- **Full Retirement Age (FRA)**—in the US, this term generally refers to the age a person must reach in order to become eligible to receive full benefits from Social Security. Early retirees (i.e., those retirees who have not reached FRA) are eligible to receive a reduced benefit. FRA depends on the year in which each person was born. It equals at least 66 years for almost all people. For people who were born before 1943, the FRA is 65 and for people born between 1943 and 1954, FRA equals 66. You can find FRA information on the

Social Security website. (For Social Security, the age of eligibility begins at 62; it can be earlier for some specific benefits.) The Social Security Administration has been increasing this age, and it might continue to increase the FRA in order to address the Social Security's solvency issues.

- **Average Indexed Monthly Earnings (AIME)** is a calculation that Social Security uses to determine a person's full retirement benefit. It equals a monthly average of earned income from the person's 35 highest earning years (up to age 60), which is indexed for wage growth. AIME depends on the person's "earnings base" (wages and self-employment income subject to Social Security FICA taxation). Indexing evens out the value of wages by taking into consideration the growth of wages over time.

- **Primary Insurance Amount (PIA)** is the second step in Social Security's calculations of the person's full retirement benefit. PIA is calculated by making adjustments to the AIME. It is based on the person's record of earnings that are taxed by Social Security. In order to have Social Security benefits grow in proportion to economy-wide average wages, Social Security annually increases the dollar bracket amounts in its PIA formula.

- **Early Benefit Reductions** are applied to retirement, spousal, or survivor benefits that a person takes before he or she reaches the FRA. For example, if a person is due a monthly 1,200 dollar retirement benefit at age 66, and the person claims benefits at age 62, then the benefit will be reduced by 25 percent (the benefit would be 900 dollars a month).

- **Delayed Retirement Credits (DRCs)** refers to an increase in a person's personal retirement benefit for every month the person waits to claim benefits beyond FRA until age 70. DRCs increase the person's benefits by 8 percent of the person's PIA annually (assuming that the person was born in 1943 or later). For example, if the person's FRA is 66 and they wait until age 70 to collect benefits, their individual benefit will max out at 132 percent of PIA. If the person is due a monthly 1,200 dollar retirement benefit at age 66 and the person defers benefits until age 70, then the person's benefit will increase by 32 percent (i.e., by 8 percent each year) to 1,584 dollars. An individual can accumulate the DRC by formally filing for a retirement benefit and suspending it (when the person suspends his or her benefit, Social Security treats the person as if he or she had filed for retirement benefits but put them on hold with the intent to restart them later.)

1. The Past and Present of the Social Security Program

In their book, Kotlikoff and his co-authors write that the Social Security program, which is a US federal program of social insurance and benefits, was created in 1935 in response to the Great Depression. It was one of many government-sponsored programs of Franklin Roosevelt's New Deal. Welfare for families without a head of household, as well as unemployment insurance, were among other New Deal inventions. From its beginning, the Social Security program was designed as a permanent program.

Today, workers who pay Social Security taxes can claim and receive Social Security benefits. Additionally, workers' spouses and some ex-spouses, as well as the disabled, widows and widowers and child survivors of deceased workers are eligible to receive Social Security benefits.

Analysis and Comments on the Past and Present of the Social Security Program

When the US slipped into the Great Depression, many politicians first thought that the Depression was just another temporary setback in the economic cycle and that the economy would get better soon. However, the Great Depression deepened. In order to deal with the problems of long-term economic insecurity, Workers Compensation programs and welfare programs for the elderly were created at the state level. On August 14, 1935, President Roosevelt signed the Social Security Act into law. In addition to Social Security, it included unemployment insurance, aid to dependent children, old-age assistance, as well grants to the states to provide medical care.

Modern Social Security benefits go beyond retirement benefits as well. They include spousal benefits, divorced spousal benefits, widower benefits, child survivor benefits and disability benefits. Because of the complexity of the Social Security System, many beneficiaries are unaware of the full scope of Social Security and all the benefits they can claim.

Today, the Social Security program is essentially a "pay-as-you-go" program. That is, today's workers pay Social Security taxes into the program and their money is used to pay monthly income to beneficiaries. This approach makes the Social Security program different from company pensions, where the money has to be accumulated in advance, and it becomes available to be paid out to workers when they retire. Company pension plans are funded in advance in order to protect the company's employees in those cases when the company goes out of business or enters bankruptcy. I will discuss in Part II of my book how the future of the Social Security program depends on the federal government's promise to keep the program solvent.

2. The Best Strategies for Collecting Social Security Benefits

In their book, Kotlikoff, Moeller and Solman propose three general rules for collecting Social Security benefits:

1. You have to be patient and postpone collecting Social Security benefits for as long as possible.
2. Get all the Social Security benefits that you can claim. (In addition to the benefits that are available to you based on your work history, you might be able to claim the benefits that are available to you through the work history of your spouse, your deceased spouse, your ex-spouse, and your deceased ex-spouse.)

3. Choose the right timing to collect Social Security benefits. For example, the system does not allow collecting two benefits at the same time. Therefore, a person can collect one benefit while the other benefit is growing.

According to Kotlikoff and his co-authors, the optimal strategy for collecting Social Security benefits is different for each household. People have the option to begin taking Social Security benefits at a certain age, which varies by birth year. (Currently, that age is around 62.) Some people should wait until the age of 70.

File and Suspend Strategy

Some people should apply for Social Security early so that their spouses, children or ex-spouses are able to collect benefits based on their work record. If they file early and exercise their option to suspend their benefit, this will allow them to accumulate delayed retirement credits, so that they can restart their benefits later at a higher value. (This strategy is permitted only between full retirement age and the age of 70.)

To be more specific, for a married couple, Kotlikoff and his co-authors think that a good strategy is to have one spouse file for the retirement benefit at age 62 and then immediately suspend its collection and wait until age 70 to start receiving their benefit. Meanwhile, when the spouse suspends collection of his or her benefits, the other spouse should then apply for a spousal benefit and collect half of the spouse's retirement benefit until the age of 70.

According to the Social Security rules and regulations, spousal benefits apply to any couple who has been married for at least 10 years, as well as to divorcees. However, spouses and divorcees have to meet certain criteria in order to claim spousal benefits. If a spouse remarries, then he or she loses spousal benefits from his or her ex-spouse. If a person gets married a few times, then the person can select from which ex-spouse the person can get the greatest divorced spousal benefit.

Which spouse should file for benefits first? The answer depends on a few factors. If spouses are of the same age, then the spouse who is a higher earner should file and suspend collection of benefits when he or she reaches full retirement age, having another spouse collecting the spousal benefit. Then, at age 70, the spouse who filed and suspended collection of benefits can unsuspend so that both spouses can collect their retirement benefits.

Waiting Strategy for Singles

Kotlikoff and his co-authors recommend that people who have never been married and for whom Social Security benefit is the only source of income during their retirement should wait to claim benefits until they turn 70. If they wait until they turn 70, then their benefits will be higher (Kotlikoff and his co-authors claim that this is true when the money is inflation adjusted).

Overall, Kotlikoff and his co-authors suggest that people consider not receiving benefits for eight years (essentially giving them away) as a way of paying a premium in advance for a higher annuity from Social Security later on. They suggest that a person should start taking their retirement benefit early only when there are serious reasons for it, such as: (1) the person needs the money; (2) the person has a serious or even terminal medical condition; (3) the person intends to make his or her older spouse eligible for a spousal benefit; (4) the person intends to enable his or her young or disabled child to begin collecting a child benefit.

Working Strategy

If a person's benefit is based on one of their previous 35 high-earning years, then the person can replace it with a higher earning year, even if it is the most recent year, in order to raise the monthly benefit. This can be done even if the person is collecting Social Security benefit and continues to work. That is, even if a person is working at the age of 90 and his or her earnings are high enough, then the person's benefit will automatically increase.

Start, Stop, Start Strategy

This strategy implies starting benefits, stopping them, and restarting benefits later. It may help those retirees who need extra income temporarily. Social Security has a provision that allows a person to withdraw his or her benefit decision within a year of making it. It requires the person to pay back everything they have received from Social Security, including Medicare premium payments. After that, the person can have a fresh start with his or her claiming record.

During the "stop" period, the person's benefits will earn delayed retirement credits. For example, if the person suspends ("stops") for the 4 years before the second "start," then their benefit will be 32 percent higher as compared to the benefit the person received right before the "stop." This strategy may help improve the benefits of the person's spouse because, in accordance with Social Security benefit rules, one spouse has to first file for retirement benefit before another spouse can file for a spousal benefit. Therefore, when a person files for retirement early, the person's benefits will be reduced, but the total income of the person's family might increase thanks to spousal benefits.

Calculations for the start, stop, start strategy can be very complicated. In order to maximize family benefits, the person and his or her spouse have to take into consideration their own age and the age of their children. People can use special benefits calculators or hire financial advisors in order to figure the best way to apply this strategy to their particular situation.

Analysis and Comments on the Best Strategies

Considering the relatively long life expectancy in the US, Kotlikoff and his co-authors use calculations in their book to show that it makes more sense to delay collecting benefits. Of course, in order to delay collecting benefits, people need other sources of income, such as 401(k) retirement funds, a job or a spouse who is still working. However, in reality, less than 2 percent of retirees wait until 70. Approximately half of Americans begin to collect Social Security benefits at age 62 simply because they do not have any other savings. Kotlikoff and his co-authors argue that such people put themselves at a disadvantage because the benefits payout is significantly higher at the age of 70 than it is at the age of 62.

In their book, Kotlikoff and his co-authors

recognize the pros and cons of working longer. They encourage people to focus on the pros and continue working as long as possible and put off receiving Social Security benefits in order to maximize their benefits. However, many people can find difficult to follow Kotlikoff's advice about working longer. Some people may not enjoy their work, and some people may no longer be physically fit enough to keep working.

In Kotlikoff's opinion, people make a mistake when they treat Social Security as an investment and try to decide at which age they have to start claiming benefits in order to get their money back. Kotlikoff argues that Social Security is not an investment. Instead, Social Security is an insurance that offers a safe payout. He compares it to homeowners' insurance. Just like people buy homeowners' insurance in order to protect themselves financially from a worst-case scenario, Social Security protects people from the worst-case scenario—living to the age of 100 and running out of money long before they die.

I would like to point out that there is a difference between Social Security and homeowner's insurance. People do not have to sacrifice their lives in order to pay homeowner's insurance. If they cannot afford it, then they can sell their house and buy a cheaper one or rent a house (or an apartment). However, ever-rising living costs, as well as ever-rising costs of medical services, are beyond people's control. To protect themselves from running out of benefits at very old age, they have to postpone their retirement and keep working.

Kotlikoff and his co-authors argue that the proposed waiting strategies offer real benefit increases, which are "over and above inflation." I disagree with their optimistic outlook on the real benefit increases because they do not take into consideration the real inflation rate. I discuss this in Part II of this book.

Kotlikoff and his co-authors further argue that their strategies can maximize people's longer-term benefit payout so that the benefits can support people until the age of 100. I can see two problems with their statement. First, the real inflation rate, which is higher than the Consumer Product Index used by the Social Security Administration, can drastically reduce people's benefits even before they turn 100 years old. Second, the Social Security program could become insolvent long before today's retirees (the primary audience of Kotlikoff and his co-authors' book) turn 100.

It is unfortunate that Kotlikoff and his co-authors do not discuss how the growing cost of medical expenses and the increasing complexity of the medical system can hinder lives of those retirees. Furthermore, Kotlikoff and his co-authors do not discuss another strategy that many Americans use today and will have to use in the future in order to max out their Social Security benefits—the "leave the country" strategy.

The "leave the country" strategy implies that retirees either permanently move to another country, where living and medical expenses are much lower than those in the US, or they continue residing in the US and travel to other countries in order to obtain cheaper medical treatment. Conventionally, some people from less developed countries used to travel to more developed countries for medical treatment. Today, many Americans are forced to travel to third world countries for medical treatments because they cannot afford medical treatments in their own country.

3. Spousal Benefits, Divorced Spousal Benefits, Widower Benefits

Kotlikoff and his co-authors advise that the optimal strategy for married couples is a joint one. They warn that the optimal benefit collection decisions made by one spouse depend on what the other spouse decides about collecting benefits. For example, a person can to take a spousal benefit only if the person's spouse has filed for his or her own retirement benefit. This is why spouses should discuss and coordinate collecting their benefits. Kotlikoff and his co-authors recommend that couples use the "file and suspend" strategy.

Kotlikoff and his co-authors warn about the

danger of *deeming*. Here is how early retirement benefit deeming might work in some scenarios. If a husband files for his retirement benefits and his wife is younger than FRA, then Social Security's rules "deem" her to file for her own retirement benefit at the time when she files for her spousal benefit. Consequently, she does not receive both of these benefits. She receives only the larger of her benefits (her spousal benefit or her retirement benefit). Moreover, both her benefits are reduced by early claiming reductions as long as she is younger than FRA. If a person waits until FRA, when deeming is not applicable anymore, and the person only takes spousal benefit, then this benefit will be equal to 50 percent of the full retirement benefit of the person's spouse.

In their book, Kotlikoff and his co-authors describe various Social Security rules and regulations that pertain to spousal benefits, divorced spousal benefits and widower benefits. Some of these Social Security rules and regulations are outlined below:

- If a person is married for a year or more and the person's spouse dies, then the person can take his or her own retirement benefit for a while, and then switch to a higher survivor benefit. (By survivor, Social Security understands a widow or widower, as well as a divorced widow or widower.) If the survivor is the higher earner, then he or she can take survivor benefit early, wait until 70, and then collect his or her own retirement benefit. (The rules for survivor benefit are complicated, and survivor benefit depends on whether a spouse dies before or after the age of 60.)

- Survivor benefit also depends on whether a deceased spouse or deceased ex-spouse took his or her retirement benefit before FRA. If the deceased spouse or deceased ex-spouse took the retirement benefit before FRA, then the survivor's benefit will be lower. If the deceased spouse or deceased ex-spouse passed away after he or she reached FRA, then the survivor's benefit equals the actual benefit, which includes delayed retirement credits that the deceased spouse was receiving. (The size of the survivor's benefit depends on the ages of spouses and Social Security claiming decisions of both spouses.)

- Child-in-care spousal benefits can be collected by surviving spouses with young children. This benefit goes up to 75 percent of the deceased spouse's PIA, and reduction penalty for collecting benefit early is not applicable in this case. If the child was disabled before he or she turned 22, then the child-in-care benefit can be collected as long as the child remains unmarried and disabled.

Kotlikoff and his co-authors point out that when it comes to a survivor's benefit, it is important to figure out the right timing of claiming a survivor benefit and a retirement benefit. For example, if your widow's benefit is higher than your retirement benefit, then the best strategy may be to take the retirement benefit as soon as possible (preferably at age 62). Later, when you reach FRA, you can collect your survivor's benefit.

In their book, Kotlikoff and his co-authors point out that the interests of people who designed the Social Security benefit rules affected the spousal benefit. Those people were men who did not want their wives to find out what they were actually earning. Consequently, the Social Security benefit rules do not allow a spouse to access an ex-spouse's earnings record, and they do not allow a widow or widower to access a late-spouse's earnings record. This restriction makes it more difficult for people to decide when they can retire.

Analysis and Comments on Spousal and Survivor Benefits

It is common to find that that people are less aware of spousal benefits than their own retirement benefits. Nevertheless, they should realize that their decision to get married can affect their benefits. If a couple does not get married, then neither person can claim spousal benefits from Social Security. When married couples look for ways to maximize Social Security benefits, they should remember that life expectancy is higher for women than for men, and men, on average, earn more income over the course of their lives than women. Kotlikoff and his co-authors point out that married couples should openly communicate with each other about finances. They should also remember that their financial situation at the age of 60 depends on the financial decisions that they make much earlier.

According to Social Security benefits rules, a divorced person can claim spousal benefits only if he or she remains unmarried. For this reason, some women who plan to file for a divorce might choose to stay married to their husband for longer than ten years. They should be warned, though, that they might be endangering their lives if domestic violence is part of their married life. Some women are also endangering their emotional well-being and integrity when they pretend to be "happily" married only in order to collect Social Security money. Kotlikoff does not seem to be concerned in his book with any moral or psychological issues related to such a strategy.

According to the National Academy of Social Insurance,

> Women are the majority (55 percent) of adult beneficiaries, collecting Social Security as retired or disabled workers, as wives, and

as widows. They make up 56 percent of Social Security beneficiaries age 62 and older, and 68 percent of beneficiaries age 85 and older. Women pay 41 percent of Social Security taxes because they earn less than men do, and they collect approximately 49 percent of the benefits because they live longer than men, on average.

According to the National Women's Law Center,

- Social Security is virtually the only source of income for nearly three in ten female beneficiaries 65 and older.
- Without Social Security, nearly half of women 65 and older would be poor.
- For 36 percent of unmarried female beneficiaries 65 and older, including beneficiaries who are widowed, divorced, or never married, Social Security

is virtually the only source of income (90 percent or more), compared to 21 percent of married female beneficiaries 65 and older.

Young women who are aware of their longer lifespans should consider working and paying into the system just as men do.

4. Disability Benefits

In order to replace their lost wages, disabled workers, as well as their spouses and dependents, can collect Social Security benefits earlier than they can collect retirement benefits. The number of people who receive Social Security disability benefits has greatly increased over the last 20 years.

Kotlikoff, who has provided expert testimony to congressional committees, asserts that Social Security benefits rules include concealed penalties, deceitful rules, as well as hidden benefits for the disabled. For example, the formula that calculates Family Maximum Benefits (FMB) is more restrictive for the disabled, as well as their qualifying children and spouses. Nevertheless, people who receive Social Security disability benefits have certain advantages:

- They can take retirements benefits early

without any reduction.

- Their disability benefits are not subjected to deeming
- Older spouses and ex-spouses are allowed to collect spousal benefits earlier.
- They can take excess spousal benefits earlier and receive spousal retirement benefit after full retirement, while their own retirement benefit keeps increasing through the age of 70.
- They can begin collecting reduced widow or widower benefits at the age of 50.

Disability benefits can affect other Social Security benefits. This is why people who wish to claim disability benefits should educate themselves about any possible consequences for their families.

Analysis and Comments on Disability Benefits

Kotlikoff and his co-authors argue in their book

that the changes in federal welfare programs introduced by Bill Clinton in 1996, caused the rise in disability payments. However, these changes might have been caused by other events and economic trends. For example, an increase in payments for disability benefits could be related to a shortage of blue-collar jobs in the US.

Overall, according to Social Security Administration data, between the start of the Great Recession in 2007 and March 2013, the Social Security Disability Insurance (SSDI) rolls increased by 21 percent. Many experts argue that this rise in disability claims was not caused by a decline in the health of Americans. Instead, they say it was caused by flaws in the SSDI program used by those people who were unable to find a job during the economic recession or were unwilling to work. If this trend continues, it might make the SSDI program insolvent, hurting those people who are unable to work due to legitimate health-based impairments.

5. Gay Married Couples Benefits

Gay marriages are not legal in all fifty states. Therefore, there are a few factors that determine if a gay couple is eligible for Social Security benefits. For example, their eligibility depends on where they were married and where the worker resides when he or she applies for benefits.

If the worker resides in a state where gay marriage has been legalized, then a claim for benefits can move forward. However, if a gay person lives and marries in a state where gay marriage is legal and then moves to another state where gay marriage is not legal, then the situation becomes complicated. It can affect child survivor benefit, widow benefits, and partners of disabled persons benefits.

Analysis and Comments on Gay Marriage Benefits

As more and more states allow gay marriage, it will become easier for gay couples to claim Social Security benefits.

6. The Earnings Test and Its Impact on Benefits

The earnings test can affect people's Social Security benefits. That is, if people choose to collect their benefits before they reach their FRA, and they continue earning outside wages (outside wage earnings include earnings in non-covered employment but they do not include investment and pension income), then their benefits can be decreased. The calculationof which income sources to use for deciding on benefits is called the earnings test. The reduction may take the form of skipped months of Social Security payments, and it is compensated with interest when the person reaches his or her FRA.

For example, if the person's FRA equals 66 and their age is between 62 and 65 (including 62 and 65), then the person's Social Security benefit will be reduced by 1 dollar for every 2 dollars of outside wage earnings that are greater than 15,720 dollars. When the person turns 66, then his or her benefit will be reduced by 1 dollar for every 3 dollars of outside wage earnings that are greater than $41,880 and that have accumulated over the months before reaching FRA. The earnings test may also affect spousal benefits if the person's outside earnings are greater than the above-described levels.

Whereas some people prefer to stop working completely because of the earnings test, Kotlikoff and his co-authors do not recommend quitting a job because of the earnings test. They explain their recommendation with the fact that the money will be repaid after the person reaches FRA.

Analysis and Comments on the Earnings Test and Its Impact on Benefits

The earnings test is usually considered as a tax on working, which discourages older Americans from working. However, in their article "Does the Social Security Earnings Test Affect Labor Supply and Benefits Receipt?" Jonathan Gruber from MIT and Peter Orszag from the Brookings Institution report that "the earnings test exerts no robust influence on the labor supply decisions of men, although there is some suggestive evidence for a labor supply response among women."

People should have savings that they can use when the earnings test reduces their Social Security. Many financial experts recommend that people have six months of savings in the bank at any time.

7. Social Security "Gotchas"

Kotlikoff warns that the worst Social Security "gotcha" is *deeming*. Deeming is the penalty for filing before full retirement age that is imposed on those people who are eligible for both retirement and spousal benefits. That is, if you take your retirement benefits before you reach the FRA, then you can be deemed (i.e., forced) to take a spousal benefit early. Consequently, your Social Security benefit becomes reduced forever. People may be lured into applying for benefits early because they want or need money as soon as possible. However, this will influence the amount of money they can collect from Social Security later because applying for benefits early decreases the amount of the benefit collected in the long run.

According to Kotlikoff and his co-authors, the

second worst "gotcha" is the following: As soon as you file for retirement benefits, you are not allowed to take any secondary benefit, such as spousal benefits, or survivor benefits, by itself. In order to avoid this pitfall, people should not take benefits at the last moment. They should take one benefit early, and then let the other benefit grow.

Kotlikoff and his co-authors warn about another gotcha; namely, the Social Security benefit statements, which are mailed to potential recipients but are not adjusted to future inflation or wage growth.

According to the Windfall Elimination provision, if a person has earned a government-agency pension at a job—which is not covered by Social Security—then the Social Security benefits that the person may have earned at other jobs (where he or she paid into Social Security), may be decreased. Upon that person's death, the person's spouse or ex-spouse will be able to collect a widow's benefit based on the earnings history of the person who died, and the government-pension offset will not reduce it. However, the widow's benefit will affect other benefits that the person receives.

Kotlikoff and his co-authors point out that there has been a slow and steady "reduction" of the benefit that surviving female spouses can in some cases claim and receive. That is, if a woman gets a retirement benefit because she has worked more and she intends to claim a widow's benefit, then the Social Security system will give her only the larger of the two benefits.

Another Social Security gotcha is that it is very difficult to understand the Social Security instructions and documentation. It is particularly difficult because of all the "jargon" used in Social Security literature. Moreover, when you need advice on your Social Security benefits, you should not trust Social Security system. Many Social Security representatives give people bad advice, making them lose lots of retirement money. If you plan to talk with them, then you have to know precisely what you should do beforehand and then insist that they take the right actions.

There is a certain limit for family-related benefits. It is called the Family Maximum Benefit (FMB). If child, ex-spouse, and survivor benefits exceed this ceiling, then payments of benefits to all beneficiaries will be reduced so that the total amount would not exceed the ceiling. A special formula used to calculate the FMB involves the amount of the primary benefit.

Analysis and Comments on the Social Security "Gotchas"

Social Security documentation related to benefits is as difficult to understand as the federal tax code. People who can afford to pay for professional services hire professionals to help them do their taxes. However, there are not that many professionals who can help people understand and maximize their Social Security benefits. This where Kotlikoff and his co-authors' book is very helpful.

Moreover, people have to be aware of numerous conditions and restrictions imposed on Social Security benefits. Some of them are listed below:

- A person has to be 62 years old or older in order to collect retirement benefits.

- A person has to be 62 years old or older in order to collect spousal benefits, and the person's spouse has to have filed for his or her retirement or disability benefit. The person who collects spousal benefits has to have been married for at least one year in order to qualify.

- A person has to be 62 years old or older in order to collect spousal benefits from an ex-spouse's earnings, and the ex-couple has to have been married for at least 10 years. Also, the person claiming spousal benefit must not have remarried. Moreover, the couple must have been divorced for at least 2 years if the person's ex-spouse is not collecting his or her own retirement or disability benefit.

- A person has to be 60 years old in order to collect widow or widower survivor benefits. If the person is disabled and did not remarry before the age of 50, then they can collect widow or widower survivor benefits at the age of 50. As long as the death was not caused by an accident, the couple had to be married for at least 9 months (this number goes to 10 years for divorced couples).

- If a person has a child of the retired worker in the person's care, then the person can collect spousal benefits at any age (there are additional restrictions that depend on the child's age).

- If a person has a child of the person's deceased spouse in the person's care, then the person can collect mother/father benefits at any age and (there are additional restrictions that depend on the child's age).

- If a person, who is either under age 18 (19 if the person is in school) or is disabled (and became disabled before age 22), then the person is eligible for child benefits for children of retired or deceased workers.

- A person has to stay married for at least 10 years in order to be able to collect spousal and survivor benefits as an ex-spouse. Social Security does not require that the couple live together for 10 years;. it only requires people to stay married for 10 years when it comes to spousal and survivor benefits as an ex-spouse.

- If a person re-marries, then he or she cannot

collect spousal benefits on any ex-spouse's work record as long the person stays remarried.

Part II. A Critique of the Principal Messages in *Get What's Yours*

1. The Future of the Social Security Program

Kotlikoff and his co-authors do not share a common vision of the future of the Social Security program. Philip Moeller is more optimistic about the program's future. Kotlikoff observes that over the long history of Social Security, the US government has been able to prevent its collapse. However, it is questionable whether the government will be able to continue making changes in order to keep the Social Security program "alive." Kotlikoff expects that people who today are 55 and older, will receive their full Social Security benefits. However, people who are currently younger than 55 will receive some limited benefits, and they will most likely have to pay higher taxes in order to receive those benefits. Paul Solman's opinion on the future of Social Security is somewhere in between.

A Guide to Kotlikoff, Moeller and Solman's

Get What's Yours

Whereas they want to think that the US government might find a way to keep the Social Security program going for many years to come, I would like to point out that the future of Social Security remains uncertain because of its solvency issues. In order to understand how Social Security can become insolvent, let's look into how Social Security benefits are funded.

The Social Security trust fund is managed by the Department of the Treasury. The fund receives money through payroll taxes, taxes on pensions, interest earnings and some other sources. When the amount of incoming money exceeds the amount of money paid in benefits, the resulting surplus is invested in "special issue" government bonds, which are not publicly traded. These bonds are kept in trust and the money goes to other government programs. Consequently, the Social Security trust fund has no actual money. It only has special bonds, which are basically a promise to repay (a bunch of IOU notes).

Do these special bonds have any real value? Will the US government be able to meet future obligations with respect to these bonds? As long as these bonds do not have any real value, they exist only as claims that will have to be financed in the future by reducing benefits, increasing taxes, and/or borrowing from the public. Furthermore, because the bonds are not publicly traded, and they exist only as the Government's promise of repayment, their reliability relies on that of the dollar.

Until 1972, the US dollar was backed by gold. Today, it is fiat money, which is only backed by the government's promise. As long as the US dollar remains the most common currency for international reserves, one can hope that the government will keep its promise to repay the "special issue" government bonds. However, should the situation change, the "Social Security" bonds might become worthless pieces of paper.

Certainly, the possibility for the US dollar to lose its status as the international reserve currency seems to be very remote. However, the US dollar has enjoyed the benefits of this special status only for a few decades (the Bretton Woods System became fully operational only in 1958). As many other economies, including the Chinese economy, are rising, one should keep in mind that change is the only constant thing in this world. Indeed, Americans have witnessed over the last couple of decades just how *un*reliable financial systems can be.

In his article, "Fearing the worst," *The Economist's* Buttonwood columnist writes,

> There have been lots of cases of paper money systems collapsing in hyperinflation (the French assignats of the 1790s, the American confederacy, the Weimar republic and so on). It is conventional to assume that modern central bankers, with their degrees and mathematical equations, will avoid this problem. But those bankers have been surprised by so many things already, from the fragility of the financial system to the soundness of the housing market, that our confidence in their wisdom should at least be shaken.

2. Social Security and Economic Inequality

In their book, Kotlikoff, Moeller and Solman discuss some well-known strategies as well as some lesser-known benefits (for example, survivor and spousal benefits). One important lesson that readers can learn from their book is that, overall, Social Security does not distribute benefits in accordance with how much people work and how much Social Security tax they pay. That is, reward is not proportional to the contribution.

For example, Social Security's spousal and survivor benefits reward with money those people who do not work and who never worked. (One can argue that a non-working spouse does work of cleaning house and cooking meals, but would not he or she have to clean his or her own place and cook meals when living as a single person?)

In Kotlikoff's opinion, Social Security

inequalities are despicable. A person who works all his or her life at a fast-food chain store and contributes into Social Security, can get much less benefit than a person who never worked in his or her life enjoying a lavish lifestyle. Kotlikoff points out that the creators of Social Security, who were older white males, incorporated such unfairness in the system when they designed it a few decades ago. That is, they designed the system that would serve their own interests before anyone else's.

As a result, single people find themselves at a disadvantage because the system offers more types of benefits to married couples. Furthermore, the system favors married couples with one earner over married couples with two earners.

Kotlikoff and his co-authors warn readers that the Social Security system is not designed to automatically award people with all the benefits they are entitled to. In order to claim all the benefits people are entitled to, they have to know and understand the complex system of benefit rules. It is not sufficient to rely on the advice from the Social Security customer representatives because some of them are not trained well enough and are not knowledgeable enough to provide people with correct information. Because many Americans are not informed enough about Social Security benefit rules, they fail to claim billions of dollars every year.

The situation with the Social Security benefits system is to a certain degree similar to that of the federal income tax system. Both Social Security and federal tax systems are extremely complicated. Those people who can afford to hire professional advisors can get the most out of the Social Security benefits system and the federal tax system, making economic inequality worse.

Kotlikoff points out that the Social Security system intentionally makes its language misleading in order to make people mistakenly think that they will get more out of the system as long as they contribute more to the system. He also observes that many secondary earners contribute to Social Security during their whole lives, and their benefit turns out to be not a penny more than the benefit they would receive if they had never worked in their lives.

3. Social Security Benefits and Real Inflation

In *Get What's Yours*, Kotlikoff repeatedly emphasizes that a great advantage of Social Security benefits is that they are inflation-proof. He writes that by adjusting benefit payouts in accordance with the inflation rate, "Social Security does a good job of maintaining the real buying power of the dollars it pays out. And this is a big, big deal."

Indeed, on January 1 of each year, Social Security increases all the benefits it is paying to beneficiaries by the rate of inflation over the course of 12 months, between the prior two Octobers. This rate of inflation is actually a commonly used version of the Consumer Price Index (the CPI), which is one of the indexes that the government uses to measure inflation. However, the US government calculates the CPI in such a way that it turns out to be less than the real inflation rate.

Let's look into how the CPI is calculated by the US government. According to the US Department of Labor, "The CPI measures inflation as experienced by consumers in their day-to-day living expenses." In other words, the government tells us that the CPI is based on consumer-spending habits, not necessarily inflation from all sources. The government lowers the CPI by altering the list of consumer products measured. For the last 30 years, the US government has changed the way it calculates the CPI more than 20 times.

Again, as long as the US government manipulates the CPI, it misrepresents the rate of inflation. The US government is motivated to manipulate the CPI and keep it as low as possible because the CPI is connected to automatic cost-of-living increases for millions of Americans, including Social Security beneficiaries, military and federal civil service retirees, etc. Moreover, the CPI does not measure any reduction in the value of money due to money creation. Obviously, the more money that is created on paper or electronically, the less valuable that money becomes.

So, what is the real inflation rate in the US? According to the Bureau of Labor Statistics, inflation is a process of continuously increasing prices. The only true measurement of inflation has to be a fixed market basket of goods and services, which includes exactly the same goods and services today as 30 years ago. The US government does not use such a fixed market basket of goods and services. Instead, the government annually changes the items in the market basket of goods and services, replacing more expensive items with different less expensive items. For example, if the price of beef increases, then it is replaced by cheaper chicken meat for the CPI calculation.

John Williams, founder of Shadow Government Statistics (also known as "ShadowStats"), argues that the real inflation rate is close to 10 percent per year. In one of his reports, he writes,

> The current US financial markets, financial system and

economy remain highly unstable and increasingly vulnerable to unexpected shocks. At the same time, the Federal Reserve and the federal government are dedicated to preventing systemic collapse and broad price deflation. To prevent any economic collapse—as has been seen in official activities in recent years—they will create and spend whatever money is needed, including the deliberate debasement of the US dollar with the intent of increasing domestic inflation.

You can notice the discrepancy between the CPI and the real inflation rate even without any complicated calculations. If you actually have to pay for various items and services, from groceries to kid's college tuition and textbooks, from your clothes to medical services, from car and home owner insurance to plumber's services—then you are aware that the price of all these goods and services increases by far more than 2 percent every year.

In his article, "If There's No Inflation, Why Are Prices Up So Much?" Michael Sivy points out at another indicator of real inflation when he writes,

> Perhaps the most telling indicator — albeit a slightly facetious one — is the Big Mac index, popularized by *The Economist* magazine. McDonalds hamburgers are available in many countries and their prices reflect the cost of food, fuel, commercial real estate, and basic labor. The price of a Big Mac, therefore, can be used to compare the economies of different countries — or serve as a bellwether of inflation in a single country. Since the recession ended, the cost of a Big Mac in the US has risen from an average of $3.57 to $4.37, or 5.2% a year.

If the real inflation rate is higher than the CPI, then middle-class wage-based buying power is decreasing and so are Social Security benefits. For example, if the real inflation rate is 10 percent per year, then a person's wage-based buying power decreases as long as the increase in the person's wage is less than 10 percent in the same year. So if the government increases Social Security benefits by, let us say, 2 percent, then the buying ability of those benefits becomes reduced as well.

If we take into consideration the real inflation rate, which is higher than the CPI, then Kotlikoff's estimate of a 76 percent increase in benefits for those people who begin collecting benefits at the age of 70 (as compared to those people who begin collecting benefits at age of 62) is exaggerated. Moreover, even a small difference between the CPI and the real inflation rate will have a significant impact on retiree benefits over time.

4. The Real Value of Kotlikoff's Book

Kotlikoff's and his co-authors' book, *Get What's Yours*, educates people about the Social Security system, providing them with comprehensive information on Social Security benefits. Their book brings to light various problems with Social Security benefits. For example, Kotlikoff suggests that to a certain extent, the US government has intentionally made Social Security rules ambiguous and complicated in order to reduce benefits. About 40 percent of the time, Social Security representatives give wrong answers to people's questions about their benefits.

Kotlikoff and his co-authors' book is limited to the current state of the Social Security benefits system, and their book does not offer any advice to the next generation of retirees who might encounter problems with Social Security solvency in the future. In their book, Kotlikoff, Moeller and Solman admit that the Social Security benefits system is very complicated and that the future of Social Security benefits is unclear. However, they write that their book is "about getting what's yours, not fixing the system or bemoaning its fate."

Their book certainly lives by its "Carpe Diem" motto, providing retirees with sound advice on how to max out their Social Security benefits today.

References

"Policy Basics: Top Ten Facts about Social Security." [the article is available at http://www.cbpp.org/cms/?fa=view&id=3261]

"Women and Social Security." [the article is available at http://www.nwlc.org/resource/women-and-social-security]

"Women's Stake in Social Security." [the article is available at http://www.nasi.org/learn/socialsecurity/womens-stake]

Buttonwood columnist, "Fearing the worst." *The Economist* [the article is available at http://www.economist.com/blogs/buttonwood/2011/03/inflation_and_doom-mongering]

Gruber, J., Peter Orszag, P. "Does the Social Security Earnings Test Affect Labor Supply and Benefits Receipt?" National Tax Journal, Vol. LVI, No. 4 December 2003 [the article is available at http://economics.mit.edu/files/6438]

Kotlikoff, L.J., Moeller, P., Solman, P. 2015. *Get What's Yours: The Secrets to Maxing Out Your Social Security*. Simon & Schuster

Sivy, M. "If There's No Inflation, Why Are Prices Up So Much?" [the article is available at http://business.time.com/2013/03/12/if-theres-no-inflation-why-are-prices-up-so-much/]

White, R. "Top 6 Myths About Social Security Benefits." [the article is available at http://www.investopedia.com/articles/retirement/08/6-retirement-myths.asp]

A Guide to Kotlikoff, Moeller and Solman's

Get What's Yours

CPSIA information can be obtained
at www.ICGtesting.com
Printed in the USA
FSOW04n2040170615
8068FS

9 781511 519168

VAULT COMICS PRESENTS

HEATHEN

NATASHA ALTERICI
WRITING & ART

RACHEL DEERING
LETTERS

SERIES COVERS BY
TESS FOWLER & TAMRA BONVILLAIN

ALTERNATE & VARIANT COVERS BY
NATASHA ALTERICI
JEN BARTEL
NATHAN GOODEN

EDITED BY
CHARLES MARTIN, REBECCA RUTLEDGE, KRISTEN GRACE

FOR CHARLES, MY GREATEST CHAMPION;
AND FOR NICOLE, MY GREATEST LOVE.

VAULT

PUBLISHER DAMIAN A. WASSEL
EDITOR-IN-CHIEF ADRIAN F. WASSEL
ART DIRECTOR NATHAN C. GOODEN
DESIGN DIRECTOR TIM DANIEL
PRINCIPAL DAMIAN A. WASSEL, SR.

CHAPTER 1

SHOW YOURSELF!

YOU SHOULDN'T HESITATE WHEN YOU'VE GOT THE SHOT.

LIV?

HEY, AYDIS.

WHAT ARE YOU DOING HERE?

WANTED TO MEET A **GHOST.**

YOU'RE SUPPOSED TO BE DEAD, RIGHT?

HOW DID YOU FIND OUT?

SAW YOUR FATHER AT YOUR GRAVE. HE PRAYED FOR THE GODS TO PROTECT YOU.

I KNEW HE WOULDN'T GO THROUGH WITH IT.

WELL THE ELDERS DIDN'T **REALLY** GIVE HIM ANY CHOICE: DEATH OR MARRIAGE?

HE DIDN'T WANT **EITHER** FATE FOR ME, I GUESS.

THOSE ARE THE ONLY PUNISHMENTS FOR OUR CRIME, AYDIS. WHAT WE DID WAS... **UNNATURAL.**

ARE YOU SAYING MY FATHER SHOULD HAVE KILLED ME?

NO, OF **COURSE** NOT, IT'S JUST...

MY FATHER OPTED FOR MARRIAGE. THE MAN IS WEALTHY AND STRONG. HE'S TAKING ME ON HIS SHIP AFTER THE CEREMONY.

I THINK IT WILL BE GOOD. I THINK IT MIGHT... **FIX ME.**

THERE'S NOTHING WRONG WITH YOU.

DON'T BE **FOOLISH,** AYDIS!

THEY'LL KILL YOU IF YOU KEEP TALKING LIKE THAT!

KLACK

HA, HA, HA, HA...

THAT'S NO ANIMAL.

IT'S CLAIMED THE LIVES OF MANY BRAVE MEN.

BRAVE MEN WITH ARGUABLY LESS NOBLE INTENTIONS.

IF SHE SURVIVES THE CLIMB, THE NEXT PART SHOULD BE EASY...

ALL SHE HAS TO DO IS JUMP.

CHAPTER 2

DO YOU THINK THE WORLD WILL END TODAY, BROTHER?

HARD TO SAY.

FEELS LIKE IT HASN'T ENDED IN A VERY LONG TIME.

CERTAINLY WOULD BE NICE IF THE WORLD ENDED TODAY, DON'T YOU THINK?

SURE, SURE.

ARROOOOOOO

MEANWHILE ON MOUNT HINDERFALL.

IT'S NOT HOT...

IMPRESSIVE NEEDLEWORK. DESIGN IS CLASSIC OF THE NORTHERN SEAFARING PEOPLE. A TRUE WARRIOR'S HELMET.

EXCEPT FOR THE ANTLERS, OF COURSE.

WHAT'S YOUR NAME?

AYDIS.

TELL ME, AYDIS; VIKING PEOPLE DON'T WEAR HORNS ON THEIR HELMETS, SO WHY DO YOU?

WELL...I HAVE THIS DRAWING THAT MY FATHER GOT FROM THE CHRISTIANS IN THE SOUTH.

THEY HAD CALLED US HEATHENS FOR WORSHIPPING OTHER GODS. SO THEY DREW US LIKE THE DEMONS OF THEIR RELIGION. WITH HORNS ON OUR HEADS.

I THOUGHT IT LOOKED PRETTY INTIMIDATING. SEEMED APPROPRIATE.

APPROPRIATE FOR WHAT?

THERE HAS BEEN NO MISTAKE. YOU PASSED THE TEST, AND CAN NOW CLAIM YOUR PRIZE.

YOU MEAN... YOU?

I DID NOT COME HERE TO CLAIM YOU. I CAME TO FREE YOU.

I KNOW THE LEGEND SAYS WHOEVER FREES YOU CAN MARRY YOU, BUT THAT'S NOT WHAT I WANT. NO ELDER WOULD PERFORM SUCH A CEREMONY ANYWAY.

WHEN WE LEAVE HERE, YOU CAN JUST... GO WHEREVER YOU LIKE. BE FREE.

IT'S NOT THAT SIMPLE.

ODIN DOES NOT LAY HIS CURSES LIGHTLY, AND MARRIAGE IS PART OF THE CURSE.

IF I LEFT THE MOUNTAIN AND DID NOT MARRY SOON ENOUGH, HE WOULD FIND OUT. I CANNOT BE FREE. I AM CURSED.

THEN I WILL LIFT YOUR CURSE.

LOOK! GOOD AS NEW. AND TO THINK I WAS GOING TO **EAT YOU**. HA HA HA!

I'M GLAD YOU'VE CHANGED YOUR MIND. YOU HAVE CHANGED YOUR MIND, RIGHT?

OH YES. LOST MY APPETITE ANYWAY.

NEVERMIND SKULL, HE'S QUITE RESTLESS THESE DAYS. MY NAME'S HATI.

I'M SAGA.

WELL SAGA, I SEE A SADDLE, BUT NO HUMAN. WHAT ARE YOU DOING OUT HERE ALONE?

ACTUALLY, I'M LOOKING FOR HER NOW. SHE WAS HEADED TOWARD THE MOUNTAINS. WHAT ABOUT YOU TWO?

WE'RE WAITING FOR THE WORLD TO END.

WHEN IT DOES, I'M GOING TO EAT THE SUN.

NO, I'M EATING THE SUN THIS TIME. YOU CAN EAT THE MOON.

WHY WOULD YOU WANT TO EAT THE SUN?

THE FIRE MAY HAVE LET YOU IN HERE, BUT I CHOOSE WHEN, OR EVEN IF WE LEAVE.

WHAT CAN I DO TO CONVINCE YOU?

YOU CAN START BY TELLING ME WHAT YOU'RE DOING HERE.

I CAME TO FREE Y--

THAT'S NOT WHAT I ASKED. WHY IS A VIKING GIRL OF MARRYING AGE NOT AT HOME WITH HER HUSBAND, OR AT HER FATHER'S HOUSE?

I KNOW YOUR PEOPLE'S CUSTOMS. YOU'RE EITHER BREAKING THEM...

OR YOU'VE BEEN CAST OUT.

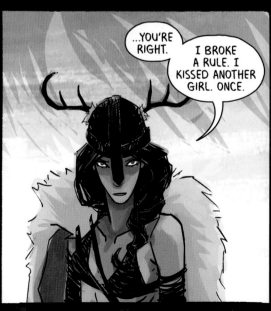

...YOU'RE RIGHT.

I BROKE A RULE. I KISSED ANOTHER GIRL. ONCE.

AS I SAID BEFORE, ODIN IS VERY THOROUGH WITH HIS CURSES.

MY BANISHMENT FROM THE GOD LANDS ISN'T JUST A WARNING TO STAY OUT.

WHEN I TRY TO REMEMBER HOW TO GET THERE, THE MEMORY BECOMES DISTORTED. I DON'T KNOW THE WAY.

BUT I KNOW WHO WOULD. WE NEED TO FIND THE VALKYRIES.

OH MY, BRYNHILD. DID YOU REALLY THINK WE WEREN'T COMING?

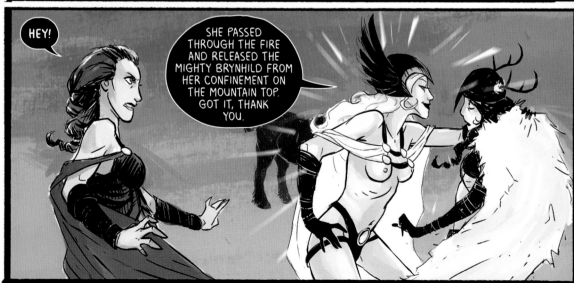

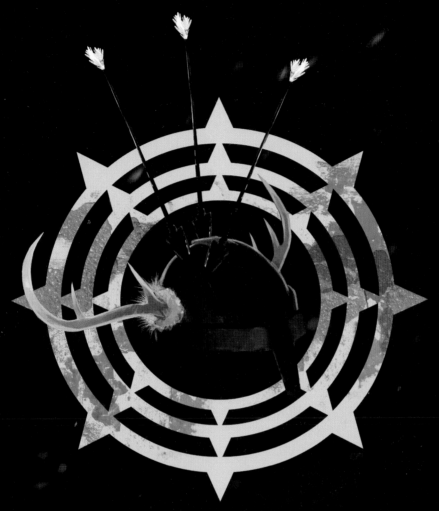

CHAPTER 3

IF IT WERE UP TO ME, SHE'D STAY FOREVER. THEY **ALL** WOULD. BUT THEY WON'T.

W— WHY?

AH, THERE'S YOUR VOICE! AND WHAT A LOVELY VOICE IT IS. LET ME HEAR MORE.

WHY? WHY CAN'T THEY STAY?

BECAUSE THEY ARE VALKYRIES, CREATED BY ODIN FOR ONE PURPOSE: TO SLAY MEN. THEY WILL SURELY BE COMPELLED TO WAR SOON ENOUGH.

EVEN NOW SHE IS FIGHTING THE URGE TO FLY OFF.

I DO WHAT I CAN TO GIVE THEM RESPITE BETWEEN BATTLES. COMFORT, REST, AND PLEASURES OF THE FLESH.

IS THAT WHY THESE PEOPLE ARE HERE? TO HAVE SEX WITH WHOMEVER YOU FORCE THEM TO?

FORCE? IS THAT WHAT YOU THINK OF ME? YOU THINK THEY'RE SLAVES?

WHAT STORIES MUST THEY BE TELLING ABOUT ME?

WELL?

FINE, THEN. I'LL TAKE CARE OF THE INTRODUCTIONS. AYDIS, THIS IS SHANNON. SHANNON, MEET AYDIS. SHE RECENTLY RELEASED BRYNHILD FROM MT. HINDERFALL. ISN'T THAT INTERESTING?

IS HE MUTE? OR IS THIS LIKE WHAT HAPPENED TO ME?

OH, NO. SHANNON HAS CHOSEN TO DENY THE WORLD HIS VOICE.

WHEN HE FIRST CAME TO ME, HE ASKED FOR MY HAND IN MARRIAGE. OF COURSE I REFUSED--MY LOVE CAN'T POSSIBLY BE CONTAINED TO JUST ONE PERSON. SO HE VOWED TO SERVE ME IN SILENCE UNTIL I CHANGED MY MIND.

NOT A SOUL HAS HEARD HIM SPEAK SINCE. MY BEAUTIFUL SILENT SHANNON.

YOU SEE, AYDIS, THE PEOPLE ARE NOT SLAVES. THEY ARE WORSHIPPERS OF LOVE, SERVANTS TO LOVE. EVERYONE IS HERE BECAUSE THEY CHOOSE TO BE.

EXCEPT FOR ME.

RIGHT, EXCEPT FOR YOU. I SUPPOSE I SHOULD HAVE STARTED WITH AN EXPLANATION FOR THAT, HMM?

YOU SENT RUADAN TO SPY ON ME. YOU WERE WAITING FOR ME TO RELEASE BRYNHILD, JUST SO YOU COULD **KIDNAP** ME? WHY?

TO **SAVE YOUR LIFE.** I'M NOT THE ONLY GOD WHO CAN SEE WHAT YOU'RE UP TO.

I'M NOT AFRAID OF THE GODS.

YOU **SHOULD** BE.

AND I'M NOT STAYING. I HAVE TO FIND **BRYNHILD.** I PROMISED TO HELP HER.

AYDIS, WAIT!

I KNOW WHERE BRYNHILD WILL BE GOING. I WILL TELL YOU, BUT I WANT YOU TO HEAR ME OUT FIRST.

TELL ME.

YOU LIKE STORIES, AYDIS. HAVE YOU EVER HEARD THE TALE OF SIGURD THE BROKEN HEART?

NO. WHAT DOES THAT HAVE TO DO WITH BRYNHILD?

SIGURD WAS THE LAST PERSON TO RELEASE BRYNHILD FROM THE FIRE.

I'VE NEVER HEARD OF ANYONE ELSE RELEASING HER.

THERE HAVE BEEN MANY OTHERS, IN FACT.

WHEN WAS THIS?

LISTEN TO ME, AYDIS. I'M SORRY I TOOK YOU FROM BRYNHILD. BUT I DID THIS NOT ONLY TO SPARE YOU FROM ODIN'S WRATH, BUT TO SPARE HER THE TORTURE OF ANOTHER LOST LOVE.

YOU WOULD DELIBERATELY WITHHOLD LOVE FROM SOMEONE, GODDESS? WHY?

BRYNHILD IS CURSED. YOU THINK IT DOESN'T PAIN ME TO KNOW THIS? I LOVE HER. SPARING HER FROM HEARTACHE IS THE ONLY THING I CAN DO TO EASE HER SUFFERING.

BUT FOR YOU, I CAN DO MORE.

FOR ME?

YES, MY LITTLE WARRIOR. I KNOW THE SECRET DESIRES IN YOUR HEART, THINGS YOU NEVER EVEN TOLD THAT PRETTY FRIEND OF YOURS ABOUT.

YOU'LL FIND NO JUDGMENTS HERE ABOUT WHO OR HOW YOU WISH TO LOVE. THIS PLACE IS PARADISE. MY HOME CAN BE YOUR REFUGE.

THAT'S NOT WHAT I WANT. I MEAN...IT IS A GENEROUS OFFER, GODDESS, AND SOME PART OF ME DOES WANT THAT KIND OF LIFE, YOU'RE RIGHT, BUT NOT FOR MYSELF.

WARRIORS DON'T FIGHT FOR THEMSELVES, THEY FIGHT FOR THOSE WHO CANNOT FIGHT ON THEIR OWN. YOU SAID YOU WANTED TO SPARE BRYNHILD HER SUFFERING? WELL, I WANT TO DO THE SAME, FOR HER AND FOR MANY OTHER WOMEN. I CAN'T DO THAT HIDING IN YOUR CASTLE.

CAN THE GODDESS OF LOVE UNDERSTAND THAT?

≤SIGH≥ SHE CAN.

SO GOOD IS YOUR HEART. I CAN SEE WHY SHE LOVES YOU.

WHO?

THERE ISN'T TIME TO GET BRYNHILD. OUR VALKYRIE FRIEND HAS GONE TOO FAR SOUTH, AND YOU, MY DEAR, NEED TO GO NORTH.

WHY NORTH?

SHANNON, I HAVE A MISSION IN SERVICE OF LOVE FOR YOU. WILL YOU TAKE AYDIS TO THE FARM AT GRETEL'S LAKE? SEE TO IT SHE TAKES CARE OF MATTERS THERE.

ALLOW ME TO GIVE YOU ONE MORE THING BEFORE YOU GO, A TOKEN TO REMEMBER WHEN YOUR STRENGTH IS WANING.

KNOW THAT YOU ARE LOVED, LITTLE WARRIOR.

COME ALONG, MY LOVELIES, YOU CAN BORROW MY HORSE. BUT DON'T GO FLYING HER AROUND. YOU'LL DO GOOD NOT TO DRAW TOO MUCH ATTENTION TO YOURSELVES.

COME, COME! WE MUST GET ODIN'S EYES OFF YOU.

TAKEN BY FREYJA? WHY?

I DON'T KNOW. BUT I HAVE TO GET HER BACK.

I WAS HOPING YOU COULD--?

BRYN. OF COURSE, I'LL HELP YOU.

THANK YOU, SIG.

I, UH... I HAVE SOMETHING OF YOURS.

CHAPTER 4

I DIDN'T SPEND ALL 300 YEARS THERE, YOU KNOW.

WHAT ARE YOU TALKING ABOUT?

THE TAVERN. I WASN'T JUST DRINKING MY TIME AWAY.

OH. WELL, THAT'S WHERE I WOULD'VE BEEN.

BUT I DIDN'T THINK THAT ABOUT YOU.

SHE'S A WITCH!

WITCHES HAVE BEEN A PART OF YOUR COMMUNITIES FOR CENTURIES. WHAT HAVE YOU TO FEAR FROM WITCHES?

ACTUALLY, BRYN, THE CHRISTIANS HAVE BEEN CONVERTING LOTS OF THESE SOUTHERN VILLAGES LATELY. THEY AREN'T EXACTLY FRIENDLY TO THE OLD RELIGIONS.

SHE'S CURSED US!

WAIT! WHAT DO YOU MEAN? CURSED HOW?

BROUGHT EVIL HERE!

CURSED OUR VILLAGE!

THE SAME SEASON SHE CAME TO OUR VILLAGE, HALF OF THE CROPS FAILED.

I SAW HER AT THE DOCKS JUST BEFORE OUR WARRIORS WERE LEAVING ON A VOYAGE. THEY NEVER RETURNED. MY HUSBAND AND SON AND MANY MEN WERE LOST!

AND SHE SUMMONED A DEMON TO POSSESS MY SON!

SHE BRINGS EVIL, WE MUST BURN HER!

NEVER REALLY HAD ANY FAMILY. LEARNED THE TRADE FROM A WITCH AS A GIRL. IT'S ALWAYS BEEN A GOOD PROFESSION. BUT OVER THE LAST FEW YEARS I'VE BEEN RUN OUT OF **ALMOST EVERY** PLACE I SETTLE.

THEY ACCUSE ME OF CURSING THINGS AND CONJURING DEMONS, CONSORTING WITH SOMEONE CALLED **SATAN?** I DON'T EVEN KNOW WHO THAT IS. I MIX POTIONS, THAT'S ALL.

I SEE. LISTEN. NO ONE'S GOING TO HURT YOU. I'M GOING TO MAKE SURE OF IT. WAIT HERE.

ONE MORE QUESTION: IN YOUR POTIONS, HAVE YOU EVER USED SOMETHING CALLED **GODSBLOOD?**

GODSBLOOD?

HOW WOULD I GET AN INGREDIENT LIKE **THAT?** I DON'T KNOW ANY GODS.

I, UH... I LIED. THERE WAS NEVER ANY DEMON.

I ASKED THE WITCH TO HELP ME, AND THAT'S WHAT SHE TRIED TO DO. PLEASE DON'T HURT HER.

THE REST OF YOU, HEED MY WARNING: THE WITCH IS NOW UNDER MY PROTECTION.

IF ANYTHING HAPPENS TO HER, I SHALL RETURN WITH THE REST OF MY VALKYRIE SISTERS AND LAY WASTE TO THIS ENTIRE VILLAGE.

AND THE BOY. HE IS UNDER MY PROTECTION AS WELL.

THANK YOU, VALKYRIE.

ANYWAY, LIV'S FATHER FOLLOWED HER THAT DAY, SO HE CAUGHT US. THERE WAS A TRIAL. NOW SHE'S BETROTHED, AND I'M OUT HERE. I CAN'T EVER GO BACK.

I DON'T HAVE ANYTHING ELSE TO LOSE. MIGHT AS WELL DO SOMETHING STUPID.

OKAY, YOU DISTRACT THE FARMER WHILE I GO INSIDE. RIGHT?

WAIT! WHAT AM I SUPPOSED TO DO WHEN I GET IN THERE? WHAT AM I LOOKING FOR?

THE ART OF HEATHEN
COVER GALLERY

FEATURING

TESS FOWLER
TAMRA BONVILLIAN
NATHAN GOODEN
JEN BARTEL

NO. 3 VARIANT
TESS FOWLER & TAMRA BONVILLAIN

NO. 2 VARIANT
NATHAN GOODEN

NO. 1 VARIANT
JEN BARTEL

NO. 2 VARIANT
JEN BARTEL

NO. 3 VARIANT
JEN BARTEL